THREE
TIMES
A WOMAN

CHICANA POETRY

Bilingual Press/Editorial Bilingüe

General Editor
  Gary D. Keller

Managing Editor
  Karen S. Van Hooft

Senior Editor
  Mary M. Keller

Assistant Editor
  Linda St. George Thurston

Editorial Consultants
  John M. Ryan
  Juliette L. Spence

Address:
Bilingual Review/Press
Hispanic Research Center
Arizona State University
Tempe, Arizona 85287

(602) 965-3867

THREE
TIMES
A WOMAN

CHICANA POETRY

ALICIA GASPAR DE ALBA
MARÍA HERRERA-SOBEK
DEMETRIA MARTÍNEZ

BILINGUAL REVIEW/PRESS
TEMPE, ARIZONA

ISBN: 0-916950-91-3

Library of Congress Catalog Card Number: 88-64101

PRINTED IN THE UNITED STATES OF AMERICA

Cover design by FORMAZ

*Photo credits: p. 2 and back cover, left—Liliana Jurewiez; p. 52 and back cover, center—Andrew's
Photography, Irvine, CA; p. 102 and back cover, right—Greg Sorber*

Acknowledgments

This volume is supported by a grant from the National Endowment for the Arts in Washington,
D.C., a Federal agency.

Acknowledgment is made to the editors of the following magazines and collections for poems by
Alicia Gaspar de Alba that originally appeared in their pages, sometimes in earlier or translated
versions:

Revista Chicano-Riqueña (now *The Americas Review*): "Easter: The Lame Bull."
Palabra nueva: Poesía chicana: Spanish versions of "La frontera," "Domingo Means Scrubbing,"
   "Madre," and "Shoes: Requiem for Ramona."
Imagine: International Chicano Poetry Journal: "Thunderbird," "Beggar on the Córdoba Bridge,"
   "Hunchback," and "Duende."
The Iowa Journal of Literary Studies: "Malinchista, A Myth Revised."
Common Lives/Lesbian Lives: "Bad Faith," "Making Paper," and "Making Tortillas."
Zonë: A Feminist Journal for Women and Men: "La frontera" (English version).
Puerto del Sol: "Shoes: Requiem for Ramona" (English version).

Acknowledgment is also made to the following magazines and anthologies for poems by Demetria
Martínez that originally appeared in their publications:

Columbia: A Magazine of Poetry and Prose (Columbia University), Vol. 13 (1988): "September."
Las Mujeres Hablan (an anthology of Nuevo Mexicana writers), El Norte Publications, 1988: "Bare
   Necessities" and "Hail Mary."
Voces (an anthology of Nuevo Mexicano writers), El Norte Publications, 1987: "An El Paso Street by
   Night" and "Crossing Over."
Tarasque II (Albuquerque United Artists), 1985: "The Arch," "May," and "January."
Midway Review 6 (Southwest Area Cultural Arts Council), 1984: "To My Goddaughter."

Contents

Preface

Three Times a Woman is a collection of the work of Chicana poets, each occupying a distinct poetic domain, each her own special and personal geography. Each has had her work published in a variety of outlets such as the *Albuquerque Journal, Bilingual Review/Revista Bilingüe, Chasqui, Common Lives/Lesbian Lives, Imagine, Iowa Journal of Literary Studies, Literatura Fronteriza, Maize, National Catholic Reporter, Palabra Nueva, Puerto del Sol, Revista Chicano-Riqueña*, and *Zonë: A Feminist Journal for Women and Men*. However, for each, *Three Times a Woman* represents publication of her first full-length collection of poetry.

Alicia Gaspar de Alba, who grew up in El Paso, Texas, and now lives in Boston, cultivates a poetry of paradox—politically, psychosexually, esthetically. Fittingly, her collection, *Beggar on the Córdoba Bridge*, opens with the poem "La frontera." Set on the Río Grande, it evokes not only the waters between two polities but between the sexes as well. The Río Grande is a woman? Or is a woman the Río Grande?

> Yo también me he acostado con ella,
> crossed that cold bed, wading
> toward a hunched coyote.

María Herrera-Sobek grew up first in Río Hondo, Texas, subsequently graduated from high school in Gilbert, Arizona, and now lives in southern California. A scholar of distinction, she has worked in the areas of Chicana literature, women's studies, Latin American literature, and Hispanic folklore. Now she adds her own poetic voice to those of her *carnalas*. Her collection, *Naked Moon/Luna desnuda*, is a poetry suffused with memories that keep alive the dead, that, with the help of ars poetica, reorder lives and events that have been blown away. Naked moon:

> Do you give yourself each night
> to some mysterious lover, or do you mourn
> the dead
> that in their quiet journey through the night
> pass by your side?

Demetria Martínez, born in Albuquerque, continues to live in New Mexico and serves as the religion writer for the *Albuquerque Journal* and as a contributor to the *National Catholic Reporter*. We always knew her work to be the product of a sensitive, caring, and committed poet. As it turned out, the folly of a U.S. Attorney caused some of the poems in her collection *Turning*, such as "Nativity: For Two Salvadoran Women, 1986-1987," to be sensitive politically as well. An attempt was made to use Demetria Martínez's poetry as evidence against her in a failed effort to prove that she conspired to violate immigration laws by helping two pregnant Salvadoran women enter the United States during the

Yuletide of 1986. The case went to court in Albuquerque in July and August of 1988, and both Demetria and Lutheran minister Glen Remer-Thamert were fully acquitted and vindicated. Not without, for yet another time, a bearing of witness to the subversive cleansing of poetry:

> Sisters, I am no saint. Just a woman
> who happens to be a reporter,
> a reporter who happens
> to be a woman,
> squat in a forest, peeing
> on pine needles,
> watching you vomit morning sickness,
> a sickness infinite as the war in El Salvador,
> a sickness my pen and notebook will not ease,
> tell me, ¿Por qué están aquí?,
> how did you cross over?

GARY D. KELLER
ARIZONA STATE UNIVERSITY

Beggar on the Córdoba Bridge

Alicia Gaspar de Alba

Alicia Gaspar de Alba   Abstract of a Life in Progress

I dropped from a two-headed tree of mexicanos on July 29, 1958—the first Chicana fruit of the family.

I grew up a few miles away from the Córdoba bridge in El Paso, Texas, surrounded by Vargases, Oliveras, Garcías, and Zúñigas. Unlike my neighbors, I attended Loretto Academy, a private Catholic girls' school where the nuns flattened your fingers with a ruler if they caught you biting your nails or scratching your crotch. In the seventh grade, we moved to the east side of town, turf of the Schreibers and the Hayses and the Petersons. In the eighth grade, my grandfather died and I had my first short story published. That was also the same year I graduated from Loretto Elementary School, a rite of passage that took me into the white, wild halls of a suburban high school where I made a name for myself as a jock, a women's libber, and a journalist.

At sixteen, I experienced another rite of passage with a young white man whom I married three years later. I also took my first bite out of Eve's apple, a flavor that would haunt me as well as my writing for the rest of my adolescence and throughout my short-lived marriage.

I took a few fiction classes in college (one with Raymond Carver, who said I had no style), but I didn't know I had poems ripening inside me until my last year at the University of Texas at El Paso. Gracias a la vida, I enrolled in a class with James Ragan, my guru of poetry, who drew out of me a deep respect for the imagery of my Mexican-American heritage.

Theresa Meléndez, my first and only teacher of Chicano literature, showed me my place in the genealogy of La Malinche and so introduced me to my identity as a Chicana.

I received my B.A. in English in 1980.

Then, in graduate school, came Leslie Ullman, my second mentor of poetry, whose philosophy of writing was "make it bare, strip it down, don't use prepositions."

I completed my Master's thesis, the first version of *Beggar on the Córdoba Bridge* with a different title, in 1983. Two years later, tired of being rejected by white editors and a Mexican lover, I decided to leave El Paso and seek higher academic enlightenment. Armed with a CIC Minorities Fellowship to the University of Iowa, I proceeded to break my heart in three places while attempting to do coursework for my Ph.D. in American Studies.

Now I live in Boston, a few miles away from the Longfellow Bridge. I traded American studies for poetry and a stable love life. My heart is healing and, despite the winter and the subway, I'm happy. I teach a new kind of freshman composition at the University of Massachusetts, Boston. I have also worked for National Braille Press, transcribing children's books into braille, a whole new experience in bilingualism. I have recently finished a collection of Mexican and frontera folk tales and am now doing research for a novel.

Publications

Alicia Gaspar de Alba has published short stories and poems in English in *Revista Chicano-Riqueña, Imagine: International Chicano Poetry Journal, Iowa Journal of Literary Studies, Common Lives/Lesbian Lives, Zonë: A Feminist Journal for Women and Men,* and *Puerto del Sol.* She has also published in Spanish in *Palabra nueva: Cuentos chicanos* (El Paso: Texas Western, 1984), *Palabra nueva: Poesía chicana,* and *Palabra nueva: Cuentos chicanos II* (El Paso: Dos Pasos Ed., 1985, 1987).

for Liliana,
gaucha who spins tangos
en mi corazón

I. La frontera

La frontera

La frontera lies
wide open, sleeping beauty.
Her waist bends like the river
bank around a flagpole.
Her scent tangles in the arms
of the mesquite. Her legs
sink in the mud
of two countries, both
sides leaking sangre
y sueños.
        I come here
mystified by the sleek Río Grande
and its ripples and the moonlit curves
of tumbleweeds, the silent lloronas,
the children they lose.
In that body of dreams,
the Mexicans swim for years,
their fine skins too tight to breathe.
Yo también me he acostado con ella,
crossed that cold bed, wading
toward a hunched coyote.

Domingo Means Scrubbing

our knees for Church.
'Amá splicing our trenzas tight
with ribbons, stretching
our eyes into slits. Grandpa
wearing his teeth.

Domingo means one of our tíos
passing out quarters
for the man with the basket
and me putting mine under
my tongue like the host.

Then menudo and Nina's
raisin tamales for dessert.
Our tías exchange Pepito
jokes in the kitchen
while we sneak a beer
into the bathroom,
believing the taste
will make our chi-chis grow.

Domingo means playing
a la familia with all our cousins,
me being the Dad 'cause I'm
the oldest and the only one
who'll kiss the Mom
under the willow tree.

After dark,
our grandmothers pisteando
tequila on the porch, scaring us
every little while: *La Llorona
knows what you kids are doing!*
'Amá coming out of the house
to drag the girls inside
pa' lavar los dishes.

Domingo means scrubbing.

Teyali's Dream

That first morning
the dream wakes her wet
and wondering
how to hide this new secret
from her grandmother.
She smells the sheets.
Tucks the corners in tightly.
Lays her uniform out on the bed.
She unbuttons her
grandpa's pajamas and lets
them fall. Elbows glued
to her ribs, she steps
up to the mirror to see
if anything's changed.
The bulbs of her breasts feel
ripe. She thinks she's grown
roots down there
overnight. Her fingers
show signs of digging.

        Voices in the garden.
        Milk bottles rattling on the porch.

She turns and snatches
up her clothes, tiptoes
naked to the bathroom, wondering
if her abuela will know,
if the dream will come again.

Madre

Every November 2nd, the day of the dead, she fills
a basket with the last yellow roses from her garden.
All year she has sheltered this rosebush from the dust-
devil wind, gold autumn blossoms for her dead:
airborne son, Spanish-born husband.

At the cemetery, her black rebozo soaks up the morning
sunlight. Rosary beads, smooth and fragile as an old
man's teeth, click in the air. My grandmother's
litany goes on for hours.

> *Dios te salve, María*
> *llena eres de gracia.*
> *Bendita tú eres*
> *entre todas las mujeres,*
> *y bendito el fruto*
> *de tu vientre, Jesús. . . .*

Kneeling next to her, I imagine Papá Carlos toothless
in his grave, making "parrot soup" with pan dulce
crumbs and coffee. Tonight, we will eat another
kind of bread, pan de muerto, rising in a Juárez bakery.

Two nights ago, it was Halloween and she prayed for all
our souls. Remember, grandfather, those Halloweens
on Barcelona Street? Your red station wagon creaking
with vampires, hunchbacks, a wolf or two digging
sugar skulls from your pockets as you drove us
through trick-or-treat.

> *Santa María, madre de Dios,*
> *ruega por nosotros. . . .*

Madre, you said, is a holy word, even if your Mamá Lupe
is superstitious. Think of Our Lady.

When Juan Diego's cloak opened to the Catholic priests,
there she was: Nuestra Señora de Guadalupe, the brown-
skinned deliverer of the new raza. Her gift,
a batch of winter roses, borne on the cloth
of her own earth-fresh image.

Lent in El Paso, Texas

blows forty days
of dust-devils

lentil soup
capirotada

and the daily litany
of wind across the city.

Afternoons, the cottonwoods
tumble like sagebrush

the ocotillos creak
like crucifixes

and women walk
with their buttocks

tucked in tight
under their skirts.

All along the border
the river speaks

in wild tongues
the voices of the penitent

ululate in jail cells
and confessionals

and women weep
for their murdered sons.

At night the litany stills
on the branches and the grass

rises again, dazed
after the whipping

but stronger and more alive.
In El Paso the wind of Lent

blows forty faithful days
without contrition.

War Cry

The tv plays late movies in Spanish.
So many voices calling back the tongue,
the curled silence of years.
One night my father stumbled over my bed.
I was three. I remember the word
he called my mother: Cabrona. Her back
a tombstone to his digging.
The blood of her newborn child
still fresh inside her, the wound
a color of ripe figs.
When he passed above me, his hand
tucked in the blanket.
The back door of the house
slapped shut. The tv played
the Mexican National Anthem:
"Mexicanos, a grito de guerra . . ."

Thunderbird

Even if you grow up around magic,

play hide-n-seek with it
in your sleep,
call it your own

invisible friend;
even if you have
listened to the great shadow

of its wings beating
against your window, a dusty red
spirit sheathing your house,

it is still a stranger.
Find it perched on a hillside
or in the lowest limb of the weeping

willow outside your door.
You can never be sure
where it's looking.

If you speak to it at all
it will vanish.
It must find *you*

alone under the night,
your blood thick with whiskey
as you carry tumbleweeds

and tarot cards
to your grandfather's grave.
If magic follows you, it will move slowly—

a yellow beak of moon
drifting over the valley,
a wet dream

spinning you into flight.

Beggar on the Córdoba Bridge

(50 pesos for a poem)

I want to keep you, old woman.
Knit your bones
in red wool, wear your eye
teeth around my neck—
amulets filled with sage.

You could teach me
the way of the gypsy:
how to dream
in an open field
(cotton or onion)
and let my hair grow long
roots in the mud.
How to take bread or fish
from the mouths of dogs,
travel bridges that are pure light,
tell the fortunes of rats.
From you, I could learn to read
the cracked, brown palm
of the Río Grande.

I want to keep you, old woman.
Weave your crow's feet
into my skin, polish
the black coins of your eyes—
currency of a higher kind.

Hunchback

(It is said that la jorobada brings good luck.
You must rub the hump gently, three times. You
must give her a coin or a piece of chocolate.)

Bent over a stone
sink in the courtyard,
she scrubs her patrona's laundry
until her knuckles bleed
indigo, beige, lavender.

By day her body is invisible
under the loose calico skirt
and shapeless huipil.
One thick braid
rides the hill of her spine
like a railroad.

Nights in her colonia, she is known
as the dream-reader. Wearing
white gauze and bracelets,
black net of hair hanging
to her knees, she peddles her visions
from house to house.

She collects gifts
of cigarettes and rum
from the men whose nightmares
she bears on her back.
Women light candles
to their favorite saints: San Judas
Tadeo, San Martín de Porres,
the Virgin of Guadalupe, but it is
la jorobada
who settles their sleep.

At home she soaks
her neighbors' dreams in a bone
basin, hangs them like wet sheets
over her eyes,
and curls up her lids.

She watches them
until their meanings grow bright
and solid as the knot in her
lucky life.

Malinchista, A Myth Revised

(It is a traditional Mexican belief that La Malinche—Aztec
interpreter and mistress of Cortés—betrayed her own
people in exchange for a new life. It is said that La Malinche
bore a son by Cortés, the first mestizo of Aztec and Spanish
blood, whom she later sacrificed when Cortés threatened
to take the boy to Spain. Some say that the spirit of La
Malinche is *La Llorona*.)

1.

The high priest of the pyramids feared La Malinche's
power of language—how she could form strange syllables
in her mouth and Speak to the gods without offering
the red fruit of her heart. He had visions of a white
man who would change her ways with an obsidian knife.

2.

La Malinche hated the way Cortés rubbed his cactus-
beard over her face and belly. The way his tongue
pressed against her teeth. She was used to smooth
brown lovers who dipped beneath her, who crouched
on the ground and rocked her in the musky space
between their chests and thighs.

3.

When the child was born, his eyes opened Aztec black,
his skin shone café-con-leche. His mother wet his
fine curls with her saliva to make them straight.
His father cursed the native seed in that first
mixed son.

4.

They slept under the black silk of a Tenocha sky,
the hammock molded around the two bodies: a woman's
buttocks heavy after childbirth, an infant weighted
by the shadows in his skull. A coyote lurking near
the river could smell their blood.

5.

The woman shrieking along the littered bank of the
Río Grande is not sorry. She is looking for revenge.
Centuries she has been blamed for the murder of her
child, the loss of her people, as if Tenochtitlan
would not have fallen without her sin. History
does not sing of the conquistador who prayed
to a white god as he pulled two ripe hearts
out of the land.

Easter: The Lame Bull

(In memory of all the Aztec souls
sacrificed during *La Conquista*)

When you kicked through the ochre door,
I knew it was over.
You dragged your back leg like a cross
through the still-warm blood
of two brothers before you.

You wanted to smash the arena
to bone fragments;
hard horns poised
as the priests of Teotihuacan.

I drank my beer slowly.
We all realized you were sick—
the way you rolled your thick, grey
tongue at the cape shadows.
You were spitting too much.

Around me, the crowd stood,
yelling, throwing dirty mats
and obscenities into the arena.
They had not come to watch sacrifice.

Picadores on bald, blind horses
drilled your back for red oil.
Young men in tight pants and pink stockings
lured you with their banderillas.
The matador did not want you.

My new beer foamed like your mouth.
Your black eyes would not close,
could not understand
what it meant to be dead.

Easter Sunday:
it is almost midnight and no one
gathers at your funeral.
Tomorrow, you will not remember
how the matador groaned
when he touched your heart
with the curved tip of his sword.

Tomorrow, I will wash bones out of my hair.

II. Bad Faith

Penance

In the churchyard a lady crawls
with pigeons to the Guadalupana.
Three men leering over their bootblacks
wax and buff the tiles with mud-
leather eyes, and they split zippers
when the woman passes with her breasts
budding from her blouse. On her knees
a street map, always bleeding, and always
the pigeons praying.

Looking at Moss

My mother walked
the carpet of her bedroom
for years. Once,
at the boney
edge of the bed
she waited for her husband
to come through the earth,
hand her a patch of moss
from his heart.
Lately, she tiptoes
through the house
pretending her life is still
hanging in the closet
where she left it to dry.
Nights in that closet,
moss creeps up
the white rocks
of my thighs.

Dark Morning Husband

You meet a woman on the street
outside a gay bar. Blonde hair,
open red shirt, nipples
like tiny fists.
She looks you over   down
the loose curve of shoulders
arms and hips. Your massive thighs
twitch in the dark.

Inside the red
glare of the dance floor,
she jams bone and muscle
against your flesh, asks you
for a light.

You take the Blonde
to her motel, watch her urinate,
help her strip
the blankets from the bed.
She tastes of menthol
and sour beer. She smells of secrets.
Her odor clings to your finger-
tips. You cannot lie.

She trembles at the way
you smash your hands
into the wall, bare your teeth.
When you leave you kick
the door. Somewhere,
a dark morning husband
waits for you to get home.

Love Rites in Marfa, Texas

(On the outskirts of a small West Texas
town, lights bloom unexplainably in the
night sky. They flare suddenly into view
and move in patterns across the horizon,
then vanish. One summer evening, five
people gathered to witness this phenom-
enon: the Marfa Lights.)

1. KEIR

Pressed between moon
and Marfa
lights, a man can fall
in love with the shapes of darkness:
four women, each a poet
sowing her own black
field of stars, words
blossoming into light.
He imagines his hands digging
the night sky, uprooting
the poem he will offer to his delight.

2. SYLVIA

She sings to God.
Her soul speaks to her in lights
that nobody understands.
The train plowing suddenly
through the mountains
is the beacon of her life.

3. DEL-MARIE

Her words touch
a flame to the silence
of dirt roads. She draws
the earth and the light
around her.

4. TEYALI

This one is unimpressed.
She hears echoes, native tongues
wailing across the land.

The burning cries
of the dispossessed.
Other ghosts flare in her eyes.

5. NAOMI

She is mesmerized
by the enigmas of the night,
strings of light
high on the mesa
picking deep desert
groans out of her heart.

Duende

At night your nails
work into the bedsheets
and the pillows.
                  You wait for me. I know
the hourglass of your bones,
your cold spine, the soft hairs
at the nape of your neck.
My fingers slide like mice tongues
along your skin;
        you are faceless.

                        Mornings,
you get up slowly. A lavender breeze
moves over the room,
over the dark
clothes of words
I cannot undress. I trace
your footprints
to the shower, the closet, the silent
stones of the typewriter.

Day after day you scratch
the liquid shade
beneath my eyelids. My lips grow
white, tremble with scars
of useless lines.
                  Tonight,
I will not be alone
with you.

Everything Is Falling Apart

nicely. Once more I trap
a spider on my mascara;

she spins eyelids where tears stop
the messages from flowing.

The party last night was a decade
of champagne and ulcers,

semen on the doorstep,
mermaids near the fire

and my own subtle suicide
attempt at making love with angels.

*   *   *

The desert vomits locusts
all day long. Out there,

through the apothecary jar
a young girl steals

crystals into the ivory of her arm.
The sand begins to blow,

to stir the insects in her hair.
She licks a popsicle with her eyes

glued to the last drop of sunlight
that does not succeed in melting

her glasses. I watch her because
it's slow, because the drug-

store is buzzing with silence.
I finger the cash box.

Often I have wanted to steal.
My arms are barely visible

beneath this sack of dry skin,
and yet I know these hands could

hurry, could scream out the front door.
Out there with the young girl

still on guard, still swarming
with her dust.

*   *   *

Everything is falling apart
so nicely, elegantly.

Trapped, at last, into consciousness,
I eat through cobwebs

and steal like sunrise
into the ivory arms of a new decade.

Leaving "The Killing Fields"

I leave the movie and the dog-eared
shadows of trees, the afternoon
light, the smell of popcorn
remind me of you, white man
stalking my dreams like Jack
and his magic seeds. At night
I hear helicopters pumping over
the roof, radio waves, the click-
click of telegrams on your pink
tongue. Wherever you are,
you must hear the same sounds,
you must remember the trench
we slept in, the hole that Alice
found, the rabbit chasing her
to a land far away from you.
Remember the eggshells littered
in the closet and my fingers
cake-sweet with blood. The cock
crowing in your belly warned you,
the gray hairs showing on your head,
the white space growing in our bed.
Five years ago I left you
wolfless: goodbye Peter, hello
Rita Mae Brown.

Today the memory of your body
looms immense, a tree trunk
sliding into the earth, into the black
mud and the blood on the car seat.
I took you between my thighs
at sixteen, the only man
who ever dropped his seeds there.
No roots, Jack, no golden eggs.
Just a slow chafing of thighs
and the taste of popcorn.

Driving Back from Ruidoso

June is the season
for dead dogs   the high-
ways of trucks and army
buses. My lover's bicycle-
rimmed eyes strain
flat fur lines   black
animal blood. I'm expecting
a blowout.
       Already,
the pines slope inward,
arrowheads   the Mescalero
mission fits tight to its postcard
hill. Up ahead,
the first dust-devils
squeeze out of the rocks,
ancient soul masters of the secret
skulls   we drag.

The Dancer

She wears veils around the house.
Enters every room
slowly, listening
to the flat, bare rhythms of her feet.
Her hands and arms
shape waterfalls in the air.

She murmurs secrets
to herself, tastes each word
like a new piece of fruit
from the garden.
She has killed Adam.
God lives inside
the birdcage in her kitchen.
Each branch lashing
against the window is a snake.

She is Salomé.
In the feast hall,
her dance weaves
seven circles of light
around her father; warms the stiff
hairs on his thighs. She wants
the head of John the Baptist.
Her fantasy involves water.

One night she folds
the top of her car, hangs
a long scarf around her neck,
goes for a drive.
As the wind rips
the red veil of her hair,
she calls out bravely: *"Isadora.
Isadora."* And the scarf
tightens on her throat
like a warm lover's hand.

Rocking

Saturday, 3 a.m.
I think of rocking
myself into a life without rooms,
wild mountain days
where I can eat sky light
and make love with women
who live in trees.

I remember you in the sierra.
Carving our names deeper
and deeper into the woods,
you said we would stay there forever.
Months later we touched in front of a Christ
whose eyelids moved.

This evening I wore scarlet:
satin nightgown tight enough
for a luna de miel.
I saw something in your eyes—
a trace of fox
tail whipping down a dark road.
The pines opened
like veins out of the ground
and you ran.

The night rocks me quiet.
An easy breeze stirs
the hairs on the inside of my thighs.
I press myself
against the cool wood of the chair
and watch you sleep,
                    knowing that soon, woman,
I will crawl into the sheets
and rock myself on the white
ledge of your spine.

Bad Faith

It's not that wild
cinnamon lips, plumfrost

cheekbones and henna high-
lights upset me.

I'm comforted
by the tubes and brushes

that paint your life.
I know you need to shape

yourself each morning
into the businesswoman

or the lady-like niece
so nobody can guess what

we do at night.
But you come home

bent, eyes and mouth
smudged

by the stories
you have told all day:

movies, Kahlúa crepes,
Sundays at the mercado

with a man who's really me.
You've named your lover

Alex, and show
your secretaries

a picture of some guy
sprawled on a Hawaiian beach.

Qué suerte, they moan,
filing their slick

vermilion nails, to be loved
by an American writer,

nine years younger
who cooks and waits

for the woman
he'll serve at dinner.

Shoes: Requiem for Ramona

(patient friend and lover
of used things)

I.

The first pair I gave you
were the *Famolare* sandals
I left under the bed one night
and found you wearing
the next morning.
You walked past me as if you belonged
to no one, as if the leather
around your toes
could keep you safe.

II.

Wind rattles
the Juárez streets, the dogs,
The Tarahumara women selling
pumpkin seeds outside the church.
I know you lie
face down on a cement floor,
bare-soled and swollen
with Cuervo Gold.
You will rise
in my shoes for the last time.

III.

At two we find you
strapped to a makeshift bed
in the Hospital General
space #43. My lover goes to the window
and weeps. At three I carry two vials
of your blood and a jar of urine
to the laboratorio five blocks
away, your last living
specimens warming my hands.
At your burial,
the woman in my huaraches
is both of us.

Ocotillo

1.

This arthritic bone
arrives here
after a lifetime of bending,
heart forked open,
dry as the chiaroscuro
of its inner light.

2.

My grandmother
has not made tortillas
in twenty years. Her
dry fingers twist
wood up to the elbows,
her whole body
creaks in the rain. I
am the last daughter
she breaks for.

3.

I have tumbled off
another desert, forked
my way into women's hearts,
swallowed their blood,
stored their pain.
Every hole in my shadow
has a name.

III. Gitanerías

i. Frenesí

In the next room one of the women I love
dances alone to a pounding disco tune.
She watches her reflection, her white,
pink-tipped breasts heaving like loaves
of bread, nothing to hold them as she spins
about the empty bed.

ii. Soledad

A young woman sits on a stranger's lawn deep
into the night, counting the numbers in her name.
She doesn't care about rapists; she fears only
herself, that force from a past life squeezing
into her wine-steeped mind, taking control,
leading her to a quick destiny of bones,
a black alley strewn with other hungry lives.

iii. Hambre

I am huddled into a short story while around me
friends are laughing and clinking long glasses
of wine. I glance up strategically and feel my
eyes puncture the still air, probe the distance
of so many faces. Someone tells me I am strangely
aggressive today, and I say *yes, I'm practicing
to be a vampire.*

I hold out my burgundy and imagine the red liquid
seeping through my teeth.

iv. Suerte

We step into the silver car and roll slowly
through the Haunted House. Our laughter
frightens us. We don't mention that we're too
old for this furtive touching of hands.

Green witches reach out of the darkness,
skeletons bow at our wheels. I lean over
and kiss your neck. Coffins creak.
As we emerge, the damp night
between our legs opens in silence.

v. Libertad

She watches the other two. One swaying in
a rattan chair, the other tangling her legs
into lotus. She knows what they need, what
she too would like to have.

Some nights when her daughter is asleep,
holding herself in the warm belly of her waterbed,
she pretends to have eased into that wet place
and feels herself drifting through a soft and
fluid love.

Past midnight, the three of them drink hot apple
tea and honey. In the middle of her kitchen,
the other two delve into each other's mouths
as she folds herself into the firm triangle
of breasts.

vi. Encanto

Two burgundy roses asleep in the white rooms
of a journal. I examine the petals, the curved,
red flesh that I never knew, that I wait for even
now. A womanhood as fresh and damp as these two
flowers rooted in my heart. Perhaps one morning
I will awaken to an insistent knocking. The door
will open by itself. And finally, without a word,
she will hand me the bouquet.

vii. Paciencia

I am a woman of the earth today. After sleeping
on an office floor, a hangover curdled thick
inside me, I rise at dawn. The first green-
gold rays spread themselves over the campus,
over the elves and witches nesting in the trees.
Another early riser moves on the street and I
wave to her, but she is not the lady I want.
I go back to the dark carpet and close my eyes,
thirsting for her voice, letting myself bleed
softly into the earth.

viii. Confusión

You know what the earth does, how it opens up
and unfolds a life. How it can break apart,
a sun-stroked puzzle in your fingers, dissolving
back into itself.

This Sunday, as you sit at home in your red robe
drinking coffee, think of all the times the earth
has given you something to unfold: a star-
tipped blade of grass, an onion, another woman's
arms. As you watch your warm body turning in
the darkness, your fingernails writing on your
flesh, remember how the soil whispers.

ix. Pasión

A woman kneads olive oil into the round flesh
of her breasts, and imagines a pair of brown
velvet eyes watching her from the bed. A haze
of Ciara perfume lingers in her hair.

It could all be so simple, she thinks, as the oil
flows from her palms, as she lifts each white
globe glistening with a strange heat. Maybe
those eyes, or the perfumed shadows of the bedsheets will hold her tonight. She will move only
when a brown hand grazes her thigh, and then she
will move forever.

IV. Giving Back the World

Gypsy: Poet Lost in a Foreign Country

(for Rita)

Even though your mother lives in Germany,
you are not at home there. You have stayed
six months without yourself, wandered
riverbanks, ferried over the Rhine,

soothed only by the slow motion of water
and the deck of cards you bury in your back
yard. You try to root yourself in the language
of family, army life, European road signs.

You have two jobs now, a vase of peach-colored
irises, but always the river calls you back.
Always you find your fingers shaping
a language of cups and pentacles on the keys

of the typewriter. You practice being firm
with yourself. Attend Christmas bazaars
with the kids, wander into neighbors' pot
luck dinners, dust the new furniture

in your home. But today you drink white
wine in a hotel room. After the second
bottle, you roam into the village, buy yourself
a sweater, an almond pastry laced with honey.

A man in a café offers to read your fortune
for six marks. The blue walls and curtains
absorb you slowly. Luminous, damp blue space
where you hold your breath and wait for the cards

to open you out of your silence. You want to start
a new language which only you will understand.
A language that speaks not of the past, not of
the firm breasts you touched like crystal balls.

A poetry that could sail far into the blood
and ease the questions congealing in your heart.
The fortune-teller says you will return
to the call of your life, carrying with you

all that does not fit in your husband's home:
a Master's degree, a woman's love tied like a yellow
kite to your wrist, the fantasy of reaching across
the ocean to a poetry that will not let go—

a root stronger than marriage or children.
You are the lone figure in the Three of Wands,
the traveler gazing at the desert ahead. You
find yourself rambling through a maze of days

and nights. Mother, captain's wife, stranger.
Even though you were born in Germany,
you are the foreigner in your home. You live
like the Mexican *Llorona*, wandering into towns,

weeping in harbors and bedrooms. She is the one
who calls that distant lover, that secret language.
The woman who haunts riverbanks, whose sharp,
birth-slow cry fills your dreams until they emerge

wet as your own thighs. You roam, gypsy, cold
as the Rhine, calling forever home. The place
where you shaped the firmest poems, the slowest
love. Your only escape now is language.

Making Chocolate Fondue

The most difficult part
is melting the chocolate.
Letting that wholeness
slip away from you
because your teeth ache
and your hangovers are just too sticky.
No matter how firm
the Toblerone is, how it breaks
in solid pieces all over
your kitchen floor,
how the sweetness clings
to your fingers and your tongue
turns hard and moist
at the thought of chewing
chocolate one more time,
you've got to melt
that stuff down.
Otherwise this recipe won't work.
And you'll never get on with your life.
You've got to line up
all your ripest memories,
arrange them like strawberries
on a pewter plate—
freeze that picture in your mind—
and let them sink

> one
> by
> one

into that sweet darkness.
Then, take your fondue fork
and throw it out the window.
You don't need more cavities.

Making Paper

(for X, 1979-86)

Tonight I wonder
at my lack of faith.

I wonder at this loneliness
stirring in my belly

like some old dragon
moving its heavy wings.

This morning the streets
were soaked in light

and the sound of bells
carried me back to the cobblestone

paths of San Miguel.
I remembered a poem, still soft

and unfinished, written to a woman
I once followed into Mexico,

thirty-two hours on a train
alone, pockets full of hope,

counting each town behind me.
How could we have known

our private journeys
had started?

You are not here
to hear the bells. The plaza

rings with children, old women
sell daisies, pottery, sun

flower seeds in salty brown bags.
I think of buying you

a glazed clay cup—morning
café-con-leche, sweet bread,

and your skin warm as the sheets
of paper I've laid out to dry

on the patio tiles. It is right
that I should make paper

out of all this dead pulp.
Give us something whole to keep.

Making Tortillas

(for Liliana, "la Argentina")

My body remembers
what it means to love slowly,
what it means to start
from scratch:
to soak the maíz,
scatter bonedust in the limewater,
and let the seeds soften
overnight.

Sunrise is the best time
for grinding masa,
cornmeal rolling out
on the metate like a flannel sheet.
Smell of wet corn, lard, fresh
morning love and the light
sound of clapping.

                 Pressed between the palms,
    clap-clap
                 thin yellow moons—
    clap-clap
                 still moist, heavy still
                 from last night's soaking
    clap-clap
                 slowly start finding their shape
    clap-clap.

My body remembers
the feel of the griddle,
beads of grease sizzling
under the skin, a cry gathering
like an air bubble in the belly
of the unleavened cake. Smell
of baked tortillas all over the house,
all over the hands still
hot from clapping, cooking.

Tortilleras, we are called,
grinders of maíz, makers, bakers,
slow lovers of women.
The secret is starting from scratch.

Letters from a Bruja

I. To My Daughter

Hija: every six years I lie
with a man,
ride his broomstick
into the dark land of my womb
(tomb of your ancestors)
and wander among the unborn
voices of your sisters.
Tonight they are agitated as fish
wives in the market
haggling for my blood.

> *I will be thin and white*, one says,
> *I shall bear you riches.*
> *I shall be big and black*, says another,
> *I shall be your warrior.*
> *I will love women*, says the third,
> *I will inherit your wisdom.*

But tonight my scorpion's blood boils
with the heat of the lion—
my half-cousin of fire,
my Aztec brother—
and you are conceived, hija,
from the worm of incest.
Already your seed bears the gift of darkness.
Already your name washes up
on the salty foam
between my thighs: Malinche,
brown woman of tongues and trickery.
Malinche, mother of the new breed.

II. To My Granddaughter

I watched you from bones
to childhood
in the crystal belly
of this glass,
saw you grow arms and legs,
fingernails and teeth,

a tiny clitoris
you would learn to play long
before your time.
I watched your tongue
wag white with that other language,
that other flag rising like a new moon
inside your soul.
The first time I heard you speak,
your voice hailed more than magic
or memories: a vision I would never draw
from my own veins, the gramarye of your blood.

And now, here you are,
ready at last for my teaching,
the first decade of your life
netted like ten crabs inside you,
each one pinching harder
at your little heart.
You ask my name, my reasons
for living alone, for singing
at midnight. You stare
at the black sacks of my breasts,
ask my why I sit in the mud
naked, why roosters eat from my lap,
why scorpions live in my mouth.

I wind stories in your native
tongue to frighten you,
but the only fear here is mine:
that innocence, that imagination
brewing me to pieces.
I am the land you left behind, little girl,
shadow of my shadow.
The woman who sold your mother
for love of Learning.
We are together only
to hunt each other down.
I have waited five hundred years for this.
In fifty more my bones will rattle
around your neck. My words will foam
from your mouth.

The Roads out of the Body

I

Yesterday I entered
myself in the mirror;
past my white tits and black hair,
I climbed
the arms of another woman,
a Malinche tree
inside me.

II

Like fish or sins
my other selves multiply
in the places of love:
la plaza, la iglesia, la Mariscal.
Some days or nights when I walk
my dog—an African dog
that doesn't bark—I see
a strange light in the trees.
Kenge has seen it before;
he is a child of the jungle.
He knows that deep in the earth
a pygmy is being reborn,
or that a pharaoh is passing
his soul to a basenji.

III

The roads out of the body
are not closed.
Tonight, we sleep by the fire,
our snake-bright skins
coiled on the earth.
Quiero gritar, she says.
Give me your tongue,
make me scream.
A sound like wild mares
on the moon.
The crush of trees
everywhere.

I have done this before.
This final loosening
of the night,
the branching off of women
and sins. My arms
crawl out wings.

Giving Back the World

Women, we crawl out of sleep with the night
still heavy inside us. We glean the darkness
of our lives from the people who loved us
as children: Abuelitas teaching us to pray,
Papás we remember in pictures, Tías and Tíos
holding our hands at the matinee.

Now, we are mothers or aunts, widows, teachers,
or tortilleras, beggars gathered in a deep
field of dreams. We offer our capacity
to grow—like hair, like night. We root
ourselves in the bedrock of our skin
and suck on the blue milk of morning.

Naked Moon/Luna desnuda

María Herrera-Sobek

María Herrera-Sobek grew up in Rio Hondo, Texas, in the Rio Grande Valley and attended elementary and junior high school there. Her family later moved to Gilbert, Arizona, in the late 1950s, where she graduated from high school in 1961. She received a B.A. degree in Chemistry from Arizona State University (Tempe, Arizona) in 1965 and worked in a biochemistry research laboratory at the University of California, Los Angeles for several years. She returned to school in 1968, receiving an M.A. in Latin American Studies from U.C.L.A. in 1971 and a Ph.D. in Hispanic Languages and Literature in 1975. She is currently Full Professor at the University of California, Irvine, where she teaches courses in Latin American literature, Chicano literature, Hispanic folklore, women's studies, and bilingual education.

Professor Herrera-Sobek has published extensively. Her book *The Bracero Experience: Elitelore Versus Folklore* (UCLA Latin American Center Publications, 1979) is in its second printing. She edited a book on Chicana writers titled *Beyond Stereotypes: The Critical Analysis of Chicana Literature* (Bilingual Press, 1985) and co-edited with Helena María Viramontes the volume *Chicana Creativity and Criticism: Charting New Frontiers in American Literature* (Arte Público Press, 1987). She has also co-edited with Professor Seymour Menton a book targeted for intermediate Spanish courses titled *Saga de México* (forthcoming, Bilingual Press). She has recently completed two book-length manuscripts titled *Mothers, Lovers, and Soldiers: Archetypal Representation of Women in the Corrido* and *Northward Bound: The Mexican Immigrant Experience in Corridos and Canciones*. Herrera-Sobek is currently doing research on the undocumented Mexican woman and on the evolution and political significance of Mexican *pastorelas*.

To my grandmother,
Susana Escamilla de Tarango
(1896-1985)
Rancho de la Soledad
Valparaíso, Zacatecas

I. Susana

Naked Moon

Naked moon
you arch your silver-white arms
through the night
in silent adoration.
Do you give yourself each night
to some mysterious lover,
or do you mourn
the dead
that in their quiet journey through the night
pass by your side?
Your arms upstretched
in grief
join the living
down below
in their
distress.

Naked moon
I sing these verses
of the dead
to you.

Susana

I'll tell the birds
Each morning when I wake
That you were here
Smiling at the dawn.
I'll tell the butterflies about your stories
Your endless tales
Of horses, river streams, and mountain pines
Of your dark heroes flying in the night
To fight the battles
That brought the morning sun.

Yes
I'll tell the bees
Buzzing in the sunlight
The moonbeams jumping
Across a darkened sky;
I'll tell the zinnias
The morning glories
And the blazing sun
That you were once
A part of time.

Grandmother

We see you
fading away
fine skin plastered to your bone
sightless eyes searching for
familiar faces
lips straining
no words
to greet
the end.

Together Again

Here we are
You and I
together again
seeing each other
through a cloud
of memories.

You
half here
half there
Me trying to close the bridge
between the two.

Near Death

Like a nightmare
I see you there
flesh hardening
vacant glance
slowly breathing
you are
in the last stretch
of a desperate journey
infinity beckoning
you crawl toward
the e-d-g-e
of life.

Death Vigil

The smell of death
surrounded your bed
One eye dead-shut
the other waiting to be closed
forever.
I sat by you and whispered
love words in your ear
but you were gone
lost between white sheets
Time
spinning its eternal web
had snared you
Long gone the light of day
You waited patiently for nighttime
to descend.

The Last Affront

A waxen doll you were
teeter-tottering
between male hands
your legs popped up
as they inserted
your grey dress
a perfect match
with your coffin.
No sound of indignation
blurted from your pursed lips
It was inevitable
that your end should be
as your beginning
a tragicomedy
played in silence.
The earth and planets
spinning mindlessly
the universe
smug in its eternity
and you there—alone—
the final remains
of your existence
primed to life
a century ago
and now
exhausted in despair
a wooden statue
creaking
ready to join the elements
in silent prayer

"Ashes to ashes
Dust to dust."

Atoms excited
at the nuptial union
of flesh to earth
You are going home
at last at last.

The grief
stuck in my throat
refuses to howl.
I do not want to
play the fool again
Enough at birth
The end shall be
in silence.

A Speck of Dust

Go ahead
talk to me
tell me where you are
don't let this barrier called life
come between us
we are but a reflection in the void
a second of pure imagination.
Go ahead move, speak
come back from the dead beyond
reaffirm my conviction
my poet's intuition
that life is
a speck of dust
whirling in the empty sky.

The Memory of You

I want
to murder the memory of you
strangle the mist you left
between the crevices
of my imagination
Blot out
Ink out
Extinguish
Exterminate
the lingering
threads
of you
hang
      i
      n
      g

    mid-air

from my grief.

Star Dust

Your remains
the remaining part of you
all that is left
all systems stopped
all vital functions ceased
Frozen, solidified,
dust will be
the future of your nerve
your verve your ecstasy
your very flesh
You have become
star dust
once again.

At the Funeral

Two women walking
carrying their grief in their hands.

Two men staring
bouncing the pain
from their eyes.

Two children playing, laughing
Life goes on.

Morning Glory

We've come to bury you
to say our last good-bye
The wind is howling in the night
The trees are braying in the dark
Nature is paying her respects
Ninety years
A lifetime of memories
You take with you
And leave behind
Where next shall we meet again?
Will I recognize you
And cheerily say
"Hello, it's good
to see you!"
Perhaps
This is the end
A brief encounter
In the universe
Life like a morning-glory
Blooming one brief moment
And then disappearing
In the night.

A Song of Death

Sing to me
a song of death
so I can comprehend
the minutes
as they tick away.

Rock the cradle
throw the stone
awake in me
the meaning of this spell.

Remembering the Dead

Remembering the dead
is like removing a
scab
beneath the hardened surface
lies
soft
pink
hurting
flesh.
The blood
ready to spurt
in excruciating
pain.

Death Wish

Death was never so sweet
as the taste of blood
gushed out
inexorably
the warmth
trickling out
cold settling in.

When You Are Gone

Yet
the daffodils will bloom
when you are gone
the eucalyptus leaves
will still rustle
when they fall
when you are gone
And all the petals of the bougainvilleas
that you adored
will still glisten in the morning sun
when you are gone.

But in the early hours
of the dawn,
I'll gently whisper your name
to let them know
that you were here
and left your smile, your tears
your anger
on this earth
but now you are gone.

II. Recuerdos/Memories

María

Before we begin
our present conversation
let me introduce
myself
My name begins with
M
M is for muerte
Dead and dying
in the tongue of ancient scribes.

The second letter: **a**
inscribes a circle
a jail
with a wing
beside it
hoping
to escape.

The **r** that follows
roars with laughter
but not too much
for in its precarious slant
the fall is steep
the hurt too painful.

And next
I should describe the
í
a peephole in the sky
inserted at the top
detached
suspended in the face
of space
entangled
in the arms of time

a particle of matter
defying gravity.
No apologies for its
insouciant bounce
away from the stake
the chain
the toil
the soil
the prisonhouse
of life.

And finally
in a coil
again
the **a**
with finality
leg outstretched
kicking in the air
ready
to mount
the wind
and fly.

No Easy Matter

No easy matter
conversing
with an absent God
He hides too well
behind insouciant clouds
His voice trails off
between the thunderstorms
and I can't hear
his mutterings
in the dead of night.
I try to catch
a phrase or two
as He rides the frothy
ocean waves
However
the sounds of riptides
muffle all He says.

I seek the desert
a perfect place
to try a dialogue.

Again
the jealous sun
obliterates His voice.

Sometimes
in the lilting lyrics
of the wind
I hear a song
but I can't comprehend
the words He sings
He must be speaking
tongues
unknown to man.

I say
and I repeat
It is no easy matter
conversing with
an absent God.

Inevitable Outcome

It was inevitable
mother
that we should end up
hating each other
I could never
compete
with the smell of
male
constant
in your nostrils.

You ran away
in search
of perfect
happiness.

I stayed
cuddled in the
dreams
of perfect motherhood.

Recuerdos

Me has robado mis recuerdos
aquellos que la abuela
guardó con todo esmero.

Intrusa
entraste por la noche
con cara de ladrón
mano de asesina
y mutilaste
para siempre
un pedazo
de mi ayer.

Sunday Mass

Sunday
was a time for misa
my wispy hand in yours
we walked the cobblestones.

"Oh dear, we are too early
the Anglo mass is on."

We wait our turn
The Mexican store
offers us quick shelter
from the onslaught
of our thoughts:
caramelos
colaciones
chocolates.

Sweet nothings
for our battered souls
It's ten o'clock
your forehead
sprinkled with
summer heat
begins to rain.

It's time to enter
the Mexican mass begins.

A house divided
by the colors of the rainbow
White Brown Black
Do not disturb the universe.
The blue-eyed God
wants it so.

Immigrants

We went from house to house
like Jews fleeing the Nazis
knocking on doors
bruising our egos
as we stooped
to beg for shelter.

Sweet Jesus
I hear their boots
pounding the pavement
of those hardened memories
One of these days
I know
the locks will fly
the steel will shatter
the wood will splinter
and all that will remain
will be
a thousand
shards
of broken Mexican clay.

My All-American Son

Watching
My all-American son
Move in and out
Of a white world
Brown skin
Glistening
In a world
That loves-hates
Brown.

Loves
Toasted
Blonde-brown
Ocean-sprayed
Sun-tanned
Oiled
Sleek
Shiny
Sun-soaked
Brown.

Fears
Earth-brown
Hawaiian
Mexican
Indian
Filipino
Brown.

Yet
The English
Tumbles
From his
American lips
Murders
The Spanish
Tongue
Slips in and out
Of a white world
With dignity and pride.

I know
His stand is precarious
One false move
And he'll be
Ejected
Rejected
Put in "his place"

American Brown
I ache for you.

Lonely Footsteps

If I write this note to
You
It is not
To remind you
You have a daughter
But because
You
Chose to walk
That lonely road alone
Aggressively pursuing
Your own song
To live for you
And you and you
Your footsteps echo
In my hurt.

The Apple

She gave her an apple
She with the blue eyes
And long blonde hair
Who wanted to kill herself.

She stretched out her
hand
With the razor-marks bracelet
Blood-red juicy apple
No knife
Just the apple.

Black-Widow Eyes

He was eighteen
She was twenty-eight
A Jewish boy
With curly brown hair.
And black-widow
Eyes.

He wanted to die.

So they made a pact
To feel life
In their lips
In their arms
In their thighs
And then die.

It didn't work
The flow between them
Kept them alive.

North and South

North Americans
Are so kind
To dogs
And cats
And trees
And bugs
And worms
And so unkind
To people.

South Americans
Are so cruel
To dogs
And cats
And bulls
And bugs
And trees
But oh so kind
To people.

III. Of Poems and Stones

Of Poems and Stones

I hate poems
They are like stones
Stones break
Words strike
Brittle on the outside
Piercing in the inside
But don't hurl them into the sky
A speck of dust
Might get in your eye.

Words

The words
Slip
In and out of my fingers
Like rosary beads
Refusing
To yield
An answer
To my prayers.

Stagnant and persistent
As the odor of hate
The question
Permeates my eyelids
With crystal beads
Breaking
Exploding
Now and then.

It isn't easy
To accept a birth
A death . . .
Impossible.

Yet
The torture lingers
Like stale tobacco
Clinging to our
Very breath.

The song continues
Its interminable
Melody
Each night
A babe is born.

Silent Scream

There is
So much pain
Inside our throats
We are afraid
That if we speak
We'll yell
We'll shriek
We'll moan
We'll scream
We'll cry
And so
We stay
Quiiiiiiiet.

A Time to Rhyme

One more verse
to drink
anonymity
sprinkled
in the forehead
of a poem
askew the meter
kick the tone
launch the verb
into infinity.
'Tis the season
to rhyme.

Slingshot

With my slingshot
full of words
I throw a verb or two.
Are you listening
Lazarus?
Rise up from the dead.
The stones
are quickly melting.

Amoebas

You really should not let
the blue sky
intimidate you
beyond the dome
of triple-celled amoebas
roars the silence
of the universe.

My Poem

I know
that my poem
will not break
the silence
Of a deaf universe
Nor stop the
thunder
of a violent storm.

No matter
the pen writes on.

IV. Tumbleweeds

Tumbleweeds I

Listen to the tumbleweeds
scratch their misery
in the desert sand.
Wind blows
and brings the rattle
of their bones
to distant eardrums.

Rain softens
their brittle pain
water heals
their wounds.

The children pray for rain.

Tumbleweeds II

Like desert tumbleweeds
We are hurled
Rolling in the infinitude
Of space and time
Our journey charted
By the incertitude
Of an absent God
We roll along our odyssey
Gathering bits of
Thorns, sticks, burrs,
Occasionally
A flower
Smiles upon us
Our bodies snap
And crumble
As the days
Grow sombre
The summers hot
The winters long
Nothing to sustain us
Except perhaps a fence or post
In which we rest
Our weary limbs
Longingly we wait
The sun's descent
A whiff of open fire
In which to throw ourselves
And for one brief incandescent moment
Light up the universe

A nova born.

The Journey

Uncurl your toes
and start to walk
the road is lean and long
the buzzards
hook their beaks
and gently bend
they bow to you
a tasty morsel.

Don't pretend
you don't know the destination
the map is marked
the blood is dripping from the cord.
Imprinted in your bones
The route is straight and clear
No detours
or stopovers.
The journey is on.

Almíbar

Remove the crust
the salt brine
from my tongue.

Almíbar, amigo, almíbar.

Rake out
the dead leaves
hanging from the pupils
of my eyes.

Once this is done
we can begin
to count
the stars.

V. A *quemarropa*

Letanía de viejas

Viejas argüenderas
Viejas mitoteras
Viejas alcahuetas
Viejas sin vergüenza
Viejas borloteras
Viejas melindrosas
Viejas mentirosas
Viejas chismoleras
Viejas huevonas
Viejas mugrosas
Viejas chapuceras
Viejas . . .

Vieja, ¿dónde están
mis calcetines?

Dios muerto

¡Qué tarea tan mezquina
me has propuesto!
Desatar los nudos
de la inteligencia.

Exponer al aire libre
el sufrimiento
encontrar razones
donde no hay razones.

Llenar el universo
de interrogaciones
pedir explicaciones
a un dios muerto.

A quemarropa

Y si el fin viene pronto
pues que venga.
No le tengo miedo al sol de medianoche
ni al viento corrompido del diluvio.
Sólo le temo a la sangre
fría que escurre del poder ajeno
que empapa al hombre con sudor lejano
de ametralladoras, rifles y cartuchos
y le impela a matar a quemarropa
al prójimo desnudo
sólo por el derecho de tener
tres mil zapatos en el closet.

Manifiesto

Con el trompo en la uña
Salgo al mundo a declararle
Que estoy dispuesta
A retar gigantes
A enamorar los vientos
A conquistar las páginas escritas
A apaciguar números ardientes
A volar con la escoba en ancas
Pero nunca
Repito nunca
A quedarme en un trono de
Cenizas.

Mariposa rosa

Sabrosa
Salerosa
escabrosa
mariposa
rosa
osas
pisarle
la frente
al mar.

Turning

Demetria Martínez

Demetria Martínez was born in Albuquerque, New Mexico, in 1960, where she attended public schools. While an undergraduate in Princeton University's Woodrow Wilson School of Public and International Affairs, she took poetry workshops. Her professors included poets Maxine Kumin, Stanley Kunitz, and Ted Weiss. She was a Wilson Scholar during her senior year and took courses in religious social ethics with Dr. Gibson Winter at Princeton Theological Seminary. Her summer work experiences included internships with the *Albuquerque News* and *Time* Magazine. She received her B.A. in 1982.

After graduating from Princeton, Ms. Martínez returned to Albuquerque. She lived at Sagrada Art Studios and began compiling her manuscript of poetry. In 1984, "Only Say the Word," a poetic drama, was performed at the Albuquerque Museum. It was later adapted for the stage and was presented in Spanish at a United Farm Workers meeting in Arizona. In 1985 she became a correspondent for the *National Catholic Reporter* and in 1986 began work as the religion writer for the *Albuquerque Journal.*

In December 1987 Ms. Martínez was indicted on charges of aiding and abetting the entry of two Salvadoran women into the United States, the first reporter to be prosecuted in connection with the sanctuary movement. In August 1988 she and her codefendant were acquitted. During the trial her poem "Nativity: For Two Salvadoran Women, 1986-1987" was used as evidence by the government. The month before her acquittal, she read with Allen Ginsberg at the Kimo Theater in Albuquerque for a Sanctuary Defense Committee benefit.

Ms. Martínez continues to reside in Albuquerque and to write for the *National Catholic Reporter* and the *Albuquerque Journal.* She has read poetry at numerous universities, including Stanford, California State University at Northridge, and Texas Lutheran College. She is the first-place winner in poetry for the 14th annual Chicano Literary Contest which is sponsored by the University of California, Irvine. Ms. Martínez is now completing a second collection of poetry.

For my grandparents:
  Luis and María Jesús Martínez
  Demetrio and Lucía Jaramillo

Refugees at the border
of a century.
The Río Grande, neck-high tonight.
Men, guns. Thunder.

The dangers are new but fear, familiar.
The old ones told us:
To find the eye of the storm
we must walk where lightning falls.

"Indocumentados."
Hunger, our one proof of origin.

Although we cry out,
we are not dying.

Too dark to see now.
Follow my voice.

I. To Keep Back the Cold

Elena at Five Years

Elena warms a brown egg
Between her palms, close to her lips,
Cold from a carton,
Chosen from the dozen.

It is the center now of a sphere
Of kitchen towels in a drawer
Next to an Amish cookbook,
Next to the oven's white side.

For three weeks at 3:15
Elena will breathe on that egg
Held between her lifelines
Against her grape-stained lips,
She anticipates the birth
Although brown eggs, her mother says,
Can't hatch.

But at 5, Elena
Has a good ear for heartbeats.
Sidewalk cracks cry
When her tennis shoe touches them,
The lava chips that embroider
The yard have names,
And a brown egg is throbbing
In the cup of her hand.

To Keep Back the Cold

1.

Squares of plastic tacked
to window frames
like fog cut to size,
huddling about our house winter long.
Hooks in walls for coats and hats,
logs stacked in the stairwell,
rags we stuff at the foot of the door.
The porch leans on its beams
like a cat braced to pounce
at the first snow swirl.

Drafts enter everywhere,
through sinkholes, floorboards.
Frost salts outlets,
night cracks and floats south
leaving kernels of ice
in every orifice.
We sprinkle kindling with kerosene,
flick the match,
flames from the mouth
of the hearth
light the path to bed,
we speak in our sleep
of keeping away the cold.

2.

Morning mounts the tents
in a refugee camp,
women stir fires with sticks,
feeding flames with whatever
their children cannot eat.
Breath claws out of sunken mouths,
a brown hand points to the sun
as if to ease the body's chill.
A woman cups her eyes,
turns from the camera,
tries to remember
the color green
as she walks this pinched

rind of earth,
a city of tarps
so starved
first winds will collapse it.

3.

In a house where 80-degree air
is delivered at the side entry,
where drapes fill up like lungs
and hold back the winds,
even here drafts leak
from mirrors, aquariums,
from pockets of woolen pants.

Parents and children tuck heads
in prayer then carve steaks
but by sunset a blizzard
balls furiously above
the oak table,
faces untraceable.
The children shatter like bulbs,
shards scuttle over carpets,
an explosion of such force
tolerates no bare flesh,
parents in goggles and boots
pick glass splinters
off the floor,
tongues frozen
to the roofs of mouths.

4.

It will take more than Einstein
to warm such a day,
and should the Salvation Army
really take over we will need more
than soup to start the thaw.
Old tricks are spent.
Like a war veteran in a wheelchair
who reads that running cures indifference,
we rip magazines
ram them between logs.
What are we to do?

Unwilling inventors in an Ice Age,
ready to burn pews.

5.

Kneel before this hearth,
listen to bark crack in the grate
as flames peak like petals.
To whom do we pray?
Against whom do we revolt
for such sorrows as a baby
frozen in a manger?
I will not sing of it,
I will not sing.
Feel ashes storm into your eyes,
you will burn
with questions of continents,
you will turn and ache
all night forever, longing
to keep back the cold.

To My Goddaughter (on her 6th birthday)

No angel beamed down
to herald your inception,
just a do-it-yourself pregnancy test.
Monday your mother and I ditched
western civ to shop for thrift store furs.
Tuesday she phoned the news. I dreamed
Wednesday night I had three breasts and
carried two eggs to an altar.
A priest cracked shells,
out fell yolk and white.

You were illegitimate as Jesus, your daddy
was no god. White friends whispered
why'd she do it?, as if your mother
had stood too long in frigid winds
and caught an embryo, as if she could
control unseemly weather with pills,
prayers, virtues timed just right.

Little raisin, you lay in a glass manger
ten days. White men came bearing oxygen
and how you shrieked. When the timer
rang we lifted you out and wondered,
will there be room for you at the inn
when winds blow and your cradle falls?
We wrapped you in a dollar-fifty fur,
carried you to an altar where a preacher
cracked jokes to make us smile,
he rocked you in water, we whispered
Amen.

Troublemaker

I want to be
a mango seed
that men trip over,
those innovators,
cradling printouts
for the production
of pink liquid soap.

Once, on a train,
I complained to a man:
we should make bread
not pink liquid soap.
He said: that's not
the American Way,
if we don't innovate
those Mexicans
will be in worse shape
than what they're in today.

I want to be a mango seed
in the street
grow into a tree
towering in the tar
to stop dead all trucks
full of pink
liquid soap.

Mother, father,
there's no passing the cup,
I'm going to be a troublemaker
when I grow up.

Hail Mary

Hail Mary
Full of grace, priests crowned you,
1598, with ruddy embers
at the village stake.
1952, your daddy knuckled you
out-of-state where unwed
mamas wheeled strollers to school.
In 1982 you were raped
red, white, and blue
by the good troops of El Salvador
who shined their rifles
at cathedral doors.

Witch. You grew herbs
to ease morning sickness,
conversed with angels.
Bitch. You made love with
life instead of a man,
birthed a troublemaker,
you asked for it.

Blessed are you among
women skimming headlines,
reading stars, awaiting
one small portent
of good news.

An El Paso Street by Night

Bronco Ballroom
Black Garter Lounge
Bueno Video
Wetbacks who scrounge
through two rusty trolleys
laid up on the tracks
touch this city's wet crotch,
you'll never go back.

Benzene dreams,
sweet sewage air,
blue motel sinkholes
choked with blonde hair.
In the next room a man
with another man's wife,
on this side of the border
she will recast her life.

She ends daylight savings,
turns back the hands,
an extra hour to fake
with this porcelain man.
Help Wanted he promised,
then fucked her backstage,
a Juárez extra scrubs sinks
at slavery wage.

Crossing

(During the 1933 Nazi boycott of Jewish
businesses, the grandmother of theologian
Dietrich Bonhoeffer crossed the line to
buy strawberries from a Jewish grocer.)

Strawberries
after supper tonight
with cream.
Like the first mother
I picked
forbidden fruit,
risking fist and boot.

No paradise, here.
The white father
in a fury lit
the pilot, split
sheep from goat,
soon ashen thunderheads
will float
over Germany.

But tonight,
strawberries.

New York Scrapbook

1.

Fog rises in shudders
from the asphalt

an old man sells roses
and lightbulbs at the curbside

the young buy tickets
for a morning pornographic flick

a blind woman tilts her face toward the sky
and knows that blue has succumbed to grey

my knapsack lumpy with camera and map
your brown face in bank windows

among the driven and the beaten
we think we know our way

with only imagined destinations
between us and them

2.

A poor black man slumps at a counter,
he wears a coat with a fake fur collar,
a Puerto Rican waitress winks,
he orders breakfast for a dollar,
she asks him: Scrambled or fried?

The old man straightens his spine,
sucks the insides of his cheeks
in serious consideration,
lifts his brows, says fried,
then smiles
because choices are rare
and sweet as sex,
that's why he eats here
that's why he loves her

Poem for the Men I Respect

I want to grow a baby in me—
Yes I do,
All I need is some loam (and seed)
And someone bold like you.

You paid my bond
You bought me beer
And took me to a play
You spoke of Locke and Hobbes and God
Then let me have my say
(We'd be thinking to a different tune
If those thinkers had been born with wombs).

You compliment me on my signs
When you see me on the news,
Demonstrating in colored hose
For justice, peace, and truth.

I'll name my baby Sophia Dolores
Because wisdom comes of pain,
You can tell the world she's yours
When I've achieved my fame.

I want to grow a baby in me—
Yes I do,
All I need is a night (or three)
With someone bold like you.

The Arch

There is an arch in my backyard
Two feet thick.
I built it brick by brick.
I shaped each block by hand
From a bucket of clay made of
Water and sand

And ground from my garden
Where weeds grew thick
Until one dry day the earth cracked
Into a jigsaw of weed root
And radish rot and so my arch
Stands on that spot.

Somewhere in that old garden
I buried a robin,
Red-breasted and jarred dead
From diving into
My bedroom window.

Now there are grey feathers
Poking out of that arch.
Little bones in the keystone
Setting under the sun.

There is an arch in my backyard
Two feet thick,
And every morning a chirping song
Sounds from between each brick.

II. *Border Wars: 1985*

Prologue: Salvadoran Woman's Lament

Nothing I do will take the war
out of my man.

A war without zones, soldiers raped
his sister at home—then disappeared him.

He returned, his rib cracked,
chest scorched with cigarettes.

The room spins at night, he says.
Last night I held him

to keep him from falling,
he called me a whore.

When at last my man gets out
to become a new man in North America,

when he finds a woman
to take the war out of him,

she will make love to a man
and a monster,

she will rise from the bed,
grenades ticking in her.

Crossing Over

". . . a sanctimonious band of renegades
who advocate open violation of the law."

> —Southwest Regional Commissioner for the U.S.
> Dept. of Justice, Immigration and Naturalization
> Service, on the sanctuary movement.
> (*Albuquerque Journal*)

1.

Somebody threw a baby
into the Río Grande.

We scrub the scum off him
in the back of the station wagon
as we leave El Paso.
We tuck him, sleeping,
in a picnic basket
as we near the check point.
Officers see our fishing rods
and nod us through.
At midnight south of Albuquerque
we invent a name, a date of birth,
singing rock-a-bye-baby in English,
burying the placenta of his past.

2.

When grandma left the Catholic Church
and joined Assemblies of God,
they dipped her in the Río Grande,
she stood up and cried.

Grandma, grandma, the river's not
the same. Sweet Jesus
got deported, this baby
bruised and hungry,
my nipples red and pained.

3.
Who's throwing babies
in the river?
What bastard
signs the release?

Who will break
the bastard's brains
and let this baby
keep his name?

"... the migration of illegal aliens to your community ...
greatly increases the cost to taxpayers of welfare and
other social programs."

Angelo's Story

A soldier told me I could find my brother
hanging from a lamppost at a bus stop
in San Salvador.

When we were boys we broke the necks
of injured birds behind the church,
I remembered this, slitting the noose.

In America I am learning to drive.
I didn't need papers to get a license.
In my sleep my brother says: go fast, go far.

Orlando's Story/The War Persists

By the time I got to San Salvador
neighbors had taken the bodies
of my mother and sister,
death squads painted silhouettes
where they had fallen.
I knew if I went to the funeral
soldiers would find me and kill me,
my grandmother told me
go north.

I have this nightmare
that started after I crossed the border,
it happened again last night.

A woman at a sewing machine
a girl in bed
ravens fly through windows
blackening the room
the woman beats them with a broom
but the birds are bullets
my mother and sister
red mouths and breasts
in circles of blood
dead.

North American Woman's Lament
(for Orlando)

1.

I, who have loved you,
paid for those bullets,
paid for helicopters above Morazán,
propellers are not petals,
nor are they wings of birds,
Bougainvillea rides the night breeze
with white phosphorus, napalm.

2.

and I thought we could love
as new creatures
that our bodies hewn together
in sleep
would stop your nightmares.

3.

A man accused me of loving
not you, but your suffering,
the story of your suffering,

making of you a myth:
this is why he left,
this is how he crossed over.

But you *are* history,
a date burnt into your chest
by the clit of a cigarette.

I know your scars as if they were my own,
a map of nations
that if grasped might deliver us

to a country where church bells
announce the time, not the dead,
where chance meetings give off light.

"My face is the face of war,"
you wrote. Invisible to those who insist
that in America all begins, new.

A handkerchief blots your alien face,
except for holes at the mouth and eyes,
reporters clip your quotes to size,

"I'm a man, not a refugee."
Newsroom clocks tally the minutes
of every country but your own,

these disappearances enrage you.
At night you come into me with vengeance,
closet light bright

because the dark, and I in it, terrify you.
Bodies cupped we fall to sleep,
stars burst blue on the T.V. screen.

4.
How your eyes hold me,
eyes where relief and fear
reside as in a cease-fire.
Your rib throbs
at my palm, the rib
they fractured with a rifle,
the rib, that if taken into the body
of America might make us new,
a country where mercy and nobility
reside, where the bones we have broken
teach us of strength.

"Grand Jury Indicts 16 in Sanctuary Movement"

(*Los Angeles Times*, 1/15/85)

An embrace, a meal, a bed,
harboring, aiding, abetting,
the night we went dancing
will be used against us,
an illicit sacrament we shared
over and over,
we, the priests
of another order
in this invisible country
called the border.

III. Love Notes

September

Night sheds her black silks,
this is the first day of the world.

Love, lover.
I uncurl your sleeping fist,

your fingers at my breast
yield up their aloes,

scars recede,
resplendent, our flesh.

No losers or victors
when wars end,

just survivors
to lay hands

on one another,
to begin again.

November

Dear B:

I read today how death squads cut off a man's
hands then shot him, children watching. I
walked in the rain to buy this card, to
forget, but look at it—the painting on it
is a lie, there is no starry night. Only
beasts disguised as men—or is it boys just
being boys? History breaks glass, makes so
little crystal. Yet I write poems, we make
love, almost with urgency, as if our little
epiphanies could alter life's molecular casing
of hate.

December

Snow, like confetti
at a parade,
a car
crumpled into a post.
Glass, glass everywhere
as if it, too,
fell
feathery
from the sky,
innocent
as infants' lashes.

A girl on a stretcher
her breasts newly budded
frozen beneath a sheet.

Tell me: how to pick glass
from blood pooled in asphalt,
how to love, our hands cut,
her life incomplete?

Glass in our bloodstream,
a generation for whom
transfusions utterly fail,
this dying called living
among machines imagined
by men who forgot
the physics of decay:
threadbare brakes,
leaks in a pesticide plant,
a wayward missile,
all they did not factor in,
the fractured face,
her father whispering
baby wake up.

January

Rosary beads
litter the headboard
useless

I ask less of heaven now
more of you

Beneath me
pinned to a sheeted horizon
you are brought to life
mouth to mouth   thigh
to thigh   true love
of true love
begotten not made
one in being.

Your face in my hands
a moon half shadowed

An astronomer
gauging your turnings
I will not lose sight
of you until sleep
fixes you in the galaxy
between my breasts.

March

Labia of amber streetlights,
women's eyes rung
with insomnia and kohl.

Lips, weathered petals,
wet with neither dew nor love,
deposits from a man's
acidic loneliness,
coins coughed up
for a quiet rape.

On these streets we hold hands
for buttressing, not love,
as once I fisted rosary beads
at a funeral to steel myself
before her white face:
perfect mother, perfect wife,
who found her audacity at last
in an act perfectly executed,
temples bored by a bullet.

Gentleness, a beatitude
unattainable
in this century,
walking these years,
night thick in our throats,
everywhere women's eyes
rung with insomnia, kohl.

May

In this parched city
drizzles are kin to monsoons.
I watch from the porch,
rain clacks on firewood
cut and stacked in February
stucco walls blush brown
as waters scrub the plaster,
branches bend to the will of the winds
that without warning deliver
your sweet scent across a continent,
telegram, urgent as death.

If I were an alchemist!
Your scent, memory distilled
with a clip of hair in a petri dish,
a flame, a prayer, you appear . . .
But we're not magicians, just lovers
withstanding the dark night:
you are, though I cannot see you,
I am, though you cannot touch me,
in these parched weeks
look how we have come to love.

July

Mugs of wine
then we walk
your dark acreage.

Dogs lap at our knees,
trees
ooze
sap,
scent of afterbirth.

Lightning
        unstitches
                the sky

Silver
    threads
            fall.

Night quickens in us
and in the crickets.

Our white bed,
your tongue
at my breast.

My
    legs
            open
                    like the beak
                bird
        great
    a
Of

IV. Turning

Nativity: For Two Salvadoran Women, 1986-1987

Your eyes, large as Canada, welcome
this stranger.
We meet in a Juárez train station
where you sat hours,
your offspring blooming in you
like cactus fruit,
dresses stained where breasts leak,
panties in purses tagged
"Hecho en El Salvador,"
your belts, like equators,
mark north from south,
borders I cannot cross,
for I am a North American reporter,
pen and notebook, the tools
of my tribe, distance us
though in any other era I might
press a stethoscope to your wombs,
hear the symphony of the unborn,
finger forth infants to light,
wipe afterbirth, cut cords.

"It is impossible to raise a child
in that country."

Sisters, I am no saint. Just a woman
who happens to be a reporter,
a reporter who happens
to be a woman,
squat in a forest, peeing
on pine needles,
watching you vomit morning sickness,
a sickness infinite as the war in El Salvador,
a sickness my pen and notebook will not ease,
tell me, ¿Por qué están aquí?,

how did you cross over?
In my country we sing of a baby in a manger,
finance death squads,
how to write of this shame,
of the children you chose to save?

"It is impossible to raise a child
in that country."

A North American reporter,
I smile, you tell me you are due
in December, we nod,
knowing what women know,
I shut my notebook,
watch your car rock
through the Gila,
a canoe hangs over the windshield
like the beak of an eagle,
babies turn in your wombs,
summoned to Belén to be born.

Blessed the Hungry

A poem for two voices
Setting: two women on a bed.

Older woman:
     A friend,
     A friend was all I wanted
     Tonight for leftovers
     Of turkey and peas,
     Home movies of a trip
     To Jerusalem,
     The twins, asleep,
     My husband abroad on business.
     Business: he intones
     That word as if it were a totem
     Against my loneliness.
     Souvenirs clatter in drawers,
     Chipped, yellow,
     Like teeth.
     Look at the blackened walls,
     We have invented fire in a house
     Where everything is flammable:
     Paper flowers, paper dolls,
     My gold ring.
     We will be incarcerated,
     Like children who light matches
     Beneath beds,
     The parent-killing types,
     We will be incinerated,
     Ashes cast to the wind,
     A curse, a sign.

Younger woman:
     Your tongue journeyed
     Down my spine,
     Like snails I let inch
     Up my shins as a child,
     Awed by the fleshy wetness.
     You kissed my lifelines,
     A blessing upon my future.
     You spread my thighs,
     In the moss found an ember,
     You breathed on it,

Coral to red, flames spreading,
Earth tremors, soles to head.
Waters of my birth canal parted
As your tongue moved in me . . .

Older woman:

Stop! A mistake, like vows
Taken in court it can be
Undone, dismissed.
A friend was all I wanted,
Joy was not intended.
The joyful dash across streets
And are hit by cars
Or by a father's fist.
Ice cubes on your thighs
Will erase the marks
Like lies erased at confession.
A mistake, unintended,
The gavel drops,
We are acquitted.

Younger woman:

Down there, down there,
My mother whispered, ashamed,
Cultures where fetuses
And illnesses fester,
Fetid, open wound
Men enter and re-enter,
Leaks and reds
On white sheets.
My first bleeding
Came like sudden death.
Each month I wore black,
Widowed, riddled with shame.

I am a virgin again, unbroken,
Brought to by your touch and scent.
Stay at my house this week or more.
We have been friends for years.
I am your sister, brother,
Mother, father.

What joyful hours rising
As lovers.

Joyful women pick themselves up
Off the street and heal
Their own wounds.
The man's tires
Flatten mysteriously in the night.
If you live with me
Our loving will split atoms,
No explosions, just additions,
New constellations
For the world to see.

Older woman:
My family, we are four,
Divisible by two,
If I lost my mind to you
My spouse and twins would be three,
Indivisible as God, a mockery.
I would lose my place
In phone books, church lists,
An outlaw, far from the sweet ache
I felt at seventeen when I took
The gold ring, unquestioning.
Veiled, I could see nothing.
Man, woman, husband, wife:
Such a comforting ordering of parts.
How it fits me.
How it makes for visibility.
I know my place
And will not touch another tree,
Even if the fruit delights,
Curiosity kills paradise.

Younger woman:
I am not ashamed
For having tasted,
At your breast
My hunger ceased.
Milk and wine: the body
Asks so little,
The mind wills gasses, acids,
Faces unhinged by blasts,

Designs for doors to stand
While houses collapse.
I want no part of such monstrous heat.
We will generate light
Like the Ner Tamid before Torah,
A flame burning in the temple,
Perpetually.
I tell you, God is pleased.
When everywhere men plan wars,
Our love is a sign,
An act of piety.

Older woman:

It is midnight, you must go,
Better that I sit in this
Big house alone.
You speak in brilliant tones,
You don't know the blacks and whites
Of children crying at night,
A husband, who in his own sweet,
Pained way, gropes for words to say
I love . . .
Three lives in my hands,
Needs to meet,
Ordinary.
I am not so proud
To want differently.
Tomorrow I wash sheets,
Skim the news, buy groceries:
Milk, carrots, chocolate, peas.
These are the little rituals
That save me from dark dissolve,
My contribution to peace.
I don't need you, I am strong,
In my own common way
I'll go on and on and on.

Bare Necessities

Coffee, scotch, 2 a.m.,
I live for revelations,

ideas foaming,
cresting into insight.

The litter of life:
books, fights, trips

Juxtaposed in conversation
so that we see the whole,

this seeing is power.

I do not live
to seek your truths for you.

Laboriously, joyfully
we come

to truth together
or not at all.

Hit and Run

Had you raped me my hate
would be radiant, sure of itself,
a memory in bruises
I could despise.
Instead we loved and sighed
from one new moon to the next . . .
then you left.

If I am pregnant I will abort,
expel you as readily as you did me,
plastic-lined can of limbs
and crushed skulls,
I, the doped-up murderess, exiting
the clinic, my insides bleached
clean, clean, what a coup,
even the getaway car awaits me.

Or, if I am pregnant, heavy with you,
a mountain, a cow, indifferent to all
but the clouds and this love
doubling inside me,
is it a girl? A head, pink and bruised,
bobs up between my thighs,
your lips and eyes,
but see how she loves me,
I am the victor here, leaving
the clinic with a pink bundle
of your best features,
your violence washed down the sinkhole
with the placenta.
Saintly, abstract:
loving you in her,
touch us and I'll
sink a knife into you, sir.

Be Still, My Heart

Be still, my heart. He does not hear you.

Be still, my heart. Women water the earth
with tears: mud into which we fall.

Be still, watch him sleep. Innocent
yet injured, he injures you in turn.

Be still, but leave his bed before dawn.

For she who waits the morning alone
will see her own face in the light.

And she who loves the light
loves the shadows that fill the earth
as she moves.

Be still, my heart. Sleep with my words.

> Adapted from "Be Still, My Heart"
> by Khalil Gibran

Bill of Rights

Leaving you violates a pact
forged between our bodies,
sealed in sweat on sheets,
notarized in letters
I pressed to my lips,
red arches over your name,
when you slit each envelope
you heard me breathing.

Leaving you: a deed of violence,
brutal as our lovemaking was ecstatic.
I do not approve, cannot condone
tearing a fetus from the womb,
a mother strangling a newborn
as famine ages her children's organs.

The fact that feeding you
meant my going hungry

My luggage, like bookends,
keeping me from collapse,
your angry sorrowful eyes,
the desire to touch
that grief compels in me,
sputtering our hatred:
more loving than silence.

The choice to survive
multiplies injuries

Against all that we promised
I choose my life over yours
I have broken the accords
I do not approve.

Divorce

I scour dead cells
with a pumice stone
off toes, ankles, shins,
scrape paint off ledges,
open windows,
watch the spider's sac
fatten on the sill.

A blue dress in a trunk
locked for years,
a blue sash to twist
about my waist,
the mirror greets me:
the woman who woke
from a coma and remembered
her name,
survivor of a wreck,
no one to blame.

Birthdays

1.

Night, with its protruding veins
of clouds

In the basement on a small bed
I dream a spider leaps from my mouth,
a woman says her blood
smells like whiskey during the hot months.

If I were rich every room in this house
would have lace curtains,
day would greet me like a new bride.

For now thank God all sorrow
has left my body,
I laugh, shivering, on red sheets.

2.

Tropic of Cancer,
I step into a quarter century,
sponging down in the shower,
carrying a cricket in the soap dish,
releasing her to the bush,
the deed that makes
all others superfluous
is what I seek.

Lining my lips brick-red,
the mirror mists with breath,
I have come to love even the mist,
the way a hand sails to the glass
to rub clear a circle for the eye.

Turning

I feel a weekend coming on
the way you feel waiting for ice cream
on a waitress's tray,
must eat slowly, let it melt
over into Monday,
Saturday, Sunday: two scoops
just aren't enough.

I think I'll walk old Nassau Street
in bare feet, gold earrings,
a Mexican dress that cost fifty cents,
I'll price paintings in a gallery,
make them think I'm out to buy,
sample perfume until I'm
ninety dollars worth of scent,
got to noon Mass, blend
with the incense, offend the ladies
with my unshaven legs: so sweet,
these weekends.

And if I catch cancer
I'll go back, buy that perfume,
make love with someone
and laugh until the end,
I've so many babies
waiting to be born.

V. *Only Say the Word*

A Poem for Three Women's Voices

"Only Say the Word" takes place at the Santuario de Chimayó, a nineteenth-century Catholic church built by Spanish colonists in northern New Mexico. In a room attached to the main sanctuary is a small hollow of earth believed to possess healing properties. Another adjoining room contains crutches, canes, and written testimonies of miraculous healings. Each year thousands visit the Santuario de Chimayó. They kneel around the hollow, cross themselves with the earth, and take handfuls home with them.

Pilgrims also venerate a crucifix called Our Lord of Esquipulas which is similar to that found at the church of Esquipulas in Guatemala. According to legend, Spaniards found the cross buried in the earth at Chimayó. Many miraculous events took place there and they built their church over that hollow of earth which is venerated today.

Long before the Spaniards built the Santuario, Pueblo Indians believed the earth in the Chimayó Valley possessed curative powers. The Indians had many legends about the area. One says that a fight between a monster and some Pueblo gods caused fire and water to emerge from the site where the Santuario stands today.

"Only Say the Word" is about three women: a Guatemalan Indian, a North American schoolteacher, and a Chimayó native.

First Voice:
    Our father who art in heaven,
    Hallowed be thy name,
    Thy Kingdom come,
    Thy will be—

    Our father who art in heaven,
    Hallowed be thy name,
    Thy Kingdom
    Come—

    How many times have I said this prayer?
    How many Sundays have the people of Cordero,
    My village, held hands at Mass
    Begging you, Lord, "Líbranos de mal,"
    Deliver us from evil?

    It does not work,
    The prayer does not work.
    The words turn to stone in my mouth.
    I must find new words

Now, or I will choke.
I must make a new prayer
The way a woman makes new soup
From yesterday's bones.

If the old prayer tires you, Lord,
Be patient.
I will salt and stir my words,
A brew so bitter,
You cannot resist forever,
You will hear, God,
You will answer.

Wood, wood and ash:
These are the colors of the people
In Cordero.
We are dark but lovely,
Strong, though now broken.
We live in shadows of guns and jeeps,
One by one we are disappeared.
Guards in green uniforms,
Like statues come to life, terrify.
After Mass one Sunday
They tore our saints out of niches,
Smashed our chalices,
Threw lots for altar cloths
Our grandmothers wove.

My husband learned to read the Bible,
He memorized the book of Luke.
After a day in the coffee plantations
Neighbors would gather to pray,
To hear my husband read:
"Bienaventurados los pobres,"
Blessed are the poor,
The Kingdom will be ours.

Then, ten men,
No older than seventeen,
The gleam of the devil
In their yellow eyes,
They beat my husband with rifles
Until his face
Was a bloody moon.

I fell on top of him,
I thought he was dead.
Neighbors' cries, like those of dogs
Tortured for fun, rose to heaven,
No guardian angels landed.

My husband lives, but cannot smell
The steam of tortillas and black beans,
Nor the scent of the body
Which bore his four children.
He calls me his "rosa,"
But what is a rose without scent?
A paper flower, flat,
Which no one will buy.
Fear, like a fruit pit,
Is lodged in my husband's throat.
He chokes in his sleep, weeps,
Speaks about escaping to the north.

Where is our help,
Christ, Messiah,
Born of a woman who made love
With life?
Must strife be our hated spouse,
Beating us?

Come down off that cross!
That thorny crown is heavy,
You have not lifted your head
In 2000 years,
Eyes closed through
Earthquake, hunger, war.
Nails at your hands and feet,
Rusty, bloody.
Your skin, brown and burnt like mine,
But you are numb.

You were once a troublemaker.
Like a woman with a broom
In a filthy house,
You whipped the temple clean
Of greedy men.
Hungry, you picked corn

From another man's fields.
Thirsty, you turned water into wine.

Come down off that cross:
Or we'll call on our old gods,
Give us this day our daily breath,
Deliver us from mad men's claws.

Second Voice:
Hail Mary, full of grace . . .
Mother to an impossible boy,
Your son's words blinded many,
His touch made the blind see.
I have forgotten how to pray.
Prayers, like nursery rhymes
And rattles, seem quaint, impotent.
A Christmas and Easter thing to do,
Like buying new shoes.
What do people say here, kneeling?
I do not know how to pray.
But I do know that when a child
Wants a favor from the father
She goes to the mother.
So I ask you, please, pray for me,
Our heavenly father has turned from me.

My student, Loretta, 15 years old,
Due in a month with twins.
I knew of her pregnancy before she did.
Conception casts a spell upon the young.
Her face grew moist,
Her sentences, fragmented.
Odors of roses, rain, came off her
As she panted into class, late.
She listened to lectures but did not hear,
Her eyes glistened like full moons.
Her essays are luminous,
She could be a scientist.
She's found a cure
For loneliness in the crucible
Of her womb.

I have taught world history
For twenty-four years.

When I was young I imagined that books
Were scaffolding about students' faces,
That teachers could restore sight.
Children might see that hate,
War, and greed are futile,
Useless as prayers to Zeus.

I'm older now, I say less,
I show slides on a screen, instead.
Of soap chunks Nazis made
With human fat,
Negatives of bodies on Nagasaki's walls,
Children's faces torn by napalm,
Their bones, little trellises
For mankind's sins.

I have taught thousands
And have helped no one.
My words, like leaves
In a fountain, decay.
What can I possibly say to Loretta,
A child turned mother
From one day to the next?

Her parents fight about money each week,
Histories of wars are nothing to her.
Valuable paintings cover the family's walls,
Like the alcohol her father consumes,
Like her mother's endless good causes:
Investments against the elements,
Loveless, sterile.
Loretta has all she wants,
Nothing she needs.

She is a fortress now,
Imperturbable.
Two hearts beating in her womb,
Two pairs of eyes and legs.
If not twins, it would be tumors
Growing, filling her empty spaces.
The body does not know the difference
When there is coldness, emptiness.

In twenty-four years
I have changed nothing.
Hope falls about me like
Chipped paint from the classroom ceiling.
At times I sit, a paralytic.
Books, teaching awards look down at me
Like disappointed parents
With nothing to say
About how to bear on.

Third Voice:

You women have wept too long
In the sanctuary,
There are tree rings around your eyes,
A ring for each year of grief.
Such wintry, leafless expressions.

You are not accountable
For the sorrows hurled at you.
A terrible rust is loose
In rain, in soil, in hearts.
Those who do not hold the gun
Are killed by the bullet,
The rest look on, indifferent.

You hold your hands
To your children's ears,
Hoping they will not hear
The terrifying report.
What more can any man
Or woman do?

Why I am blessed with safety,
With happiness, I do not know.
I was baptized, confirmed
And married at this altar.
The town of Chimayó
Is as familiar to me as water.
My husband and boy raise cattle,
We run a small store.

I sat in bed last night by an open window,
Watching cottonwoods collect
Stars in leafy nets.

Scents of sweet grass and hay
From my husband's body filled me.
I walked along the road this morning,
Sunlight turned Chimayó's stuccoed walls
Into copper and gold.
My grey hairs turned gold.
I am rich, very rich:
No boot has kicked open my door at night,
Sadness does not splinter my heart.

Each year thousands visit this church.
During Holy Week by car, on foot,
Like salmon twisting upstream
Returning to the place of birth, they come:
Cold, easterly winds cannot stop them.
Purses, pockets swell with rosaries
And plastic bags.
They hear Mass, they line up
To enter the room with "la tierra bendita,"
A room with a pit of sacred earth.
They place it on their tongues
And in bags to take home.
Stories of miraculous healings
Are strewn about like seeds in wind.
Each year a few more crutches and canes
Hang from hooks on the wall,
Useless as old calendars.

Something happens to people in this church,
Though they themselves do not always see it.
Hair and skin smell of incense, candle wax,
Eyes, like lakes on a still day,
Look to the sun, unflinching.
Praying can alter the body
As much as the soul.
Lines that life chisels into faces
For a moment fade.
They may not know it
But they have made love.

I have said enough.
You women must enter the room,
And kneel before the sacred pit.
It is dark but lovely.

Like the *sipapu* of a Pueblo Kiva,
It is a hole leading
To the center of the earth.
Once it yielded fire and smoke.
It grows larger as you look,
Like a woman dilating before birth.

Rub the earth into your palms,
Scars on your lifelines will fade.
Rub the earth into your lips,
Your words will emblazon neighbor and student,
As for your enemies, your wisdom
Is poison.
Come in now: It is sin to think all is hopeless,
Those who say you are helpless will die.

First Voice:
I am afraid to enter,
The door is narrow,
I am years pregnant with grief.
My healing has no meaning
When around me thousands
Are missing, dying.

What cure can come to us now?
When we are hungry
Bishops tell us to pray.
Thirsty, we cross ourselves with Holy Water
While armies seize our lands.
Our neighbors' naked bodies
Turn up in fields after rain.
Our children neither read nor write
But beg before cathedral doors.

Second Voice:
I am afraid to enter,
The door is narrow,
I am heavy with despair.
Blizzards are predicted this year,
How will my students
Find their way home?
Latitudes, longitudes,
Maps I use in class
Give direction to no one.

There is no progress,
Just a broken compass,
In such icy whiteness
Not a thing I can do.

I hunger, but not for food.
Thirst, but not for brandy.
In the pit of my being
I am cold, so cold,
Yet I wear fine woolen clothes.
These days I hardly smile or speak,
I earn a living but cannot live.

Third Voice:
I am exposed, unclothed.
See me for what I am,
What we all are:
A woman with no answers,
Only stories to tell.
Answers elude me like
Dollar bills in the wind.
Quarters in my pockets
To buy stamps,
Stories to tell grandchildren:
These are enough for me,
These are my only certainties.

Ten years ago in the dirt lot
In front of the church,
A seventeen-year-old girl stood,
Writing in a green notebook.
She looked at the twin towers,
Transfixed, as if painting,
As if seeing a miracle.
All I remember next were shouts,
Dust, a wreath of people
Around the girl's body.
The car that backed into her
Reflected the noon sun,
Blinding me.

The girl was my daughter,
She longed to be a writer.
In September she was to leave home

For Harvard, the first of our family
To go away to school.
All her fingers were broken,
Her life, taken.
In her green notebook,
A poem, half-written.

For weeks I could not speak.
I went to Mass daily
The way a mad woman continues to go
To a well where she drew water all her life,
Although the well is now dry.
I could not stand or kneel
Or make the sign of the cross.
Withered roses from my girl's funeral
Adorned the altar.
When Father Romero lifted the host
It became a moon with my daughter's face.
The only prayer I could say:
"Una palabra tuya bastará para sanarme."
Only say the word
And I shall be healed.

At home I fingered my rosary
Into the reaches of the night,
I burned candles before my painting
Of the Virgin,
I prayed until sleep blurred my words
Into another language.
At a time when I had no faith left,
The only thing left was faith.

One dawn, after many nightmares,
I had a dream:
I planted seeds
In my girl's bedroom carpet,
I waited for blossoms,
Nothing happened.
I opened a curtain,
An oval of light so brilliant
I could hardly look,
Fell upon the floor.
In the oval sat a baby,
Her skin dark as burnt wood,

She had no right arm.
Seeds and earth
In her left fist
Trickled into the carpet.
Before I woke up,
Three fruit trees
Touched the ceiling,
Lemon, orange, lime.

Next morning, for the first time
In memory I heard the words at Mass,
I knelt, stood, and sang.

It is growing late, cold,
You are tired.
Forgive me.
From where you stand my dreams
Are tinsel on a dead tree.
You are hungry, thirsty,
Asking why?
Ask loudly enough and that question
Will fracture nations,
Repeat yourselves, like bells on Sunday.
Some will awaken and join you,
Someone will try to kill you.

I have held hands with women
Shouting at birth,
Shouting in black at burials.
Each time I think,
God is bound to hear,
God is bound to answer.

Second Voice:
    Before I leave
    I will rub my lifelines
    With earth from the pit.
    If I can point a way for Loretta
    To take through this blizzard,
    Even if I stay behind,
    Maybe,
    Maybe there is hope.

First Voice:
        Before I leave
        I will touch my lips
        With earth from the pit.
        If I can shout louder
        Than rifle fire,
        Even if the rifle is aimed at me,
        Maybe, maybe . . .

Third Voice:
        Too dark for you to leave,
        Stay at my house tonight.
        At least for this night
        You will sleep warmly,
        Like women who have just given birth.
        The child you nurse
        Does not yet have a name.
        But when you wake up you will know.
        In dreams you will see
        What the name must be.